St Antholin's Lectureship
Charity Lecture 2016

Portrait of a Prophet

Lessons from the Preaching of John Owen (1616–1683)

Martyn C. Cowan

Portrait of a Prophet: Lessons from the Preaching of John Owen (1616-1683)© Martyn C. Cowan 2016

ISBN 978-1-906327-41-5

Cover photo: detail from 'The Popish Damnable Plot' [London, Baldwin: 1680] © Trustees of the British Museum, showing a cleric preaching to a congregation during one of the 'national days of humiliation' (13 November 1678 and 11 April 1679, as decreed by royal proclamation).

Published by the Latimer Trust June 2016

The Latimer Trust (formerly Latimer House, Oxford) is a conservative Evangelical research organisation within the Church of England, whose main aim is to promote the history and theology of Anglicanism as understood by those in the Reformed tradition. Interested readers are welcome to consult its website for further details of its many activities.

The Latimer Trust
c/o Oak Hill College
London N14 4PS UK
Registered Charity: 1084337
Company Number: 4104465
Web: www.latimertrust.org
E-mail: administrator@latimertrust.org

Views expressed in works published by The Latimer Trust are those of the authors and do not necessarily represent the official position of The Latimer Trust.

CONTENTS

1. Introduction 1
2. John Owen's prophetic preaching 4
    2.1. Preaching to those uniquely blessed 6
    2.2. Preaching to those obligated to respond 9
    2.3. Preaching to those consistently negligent 13
    2.4. Preaching to those warned by judgment 22
3. Conclusion 31

St. Antholin's Lectureship Charity Lectures 35

1. Introduction

John Owen was convinced that history is full of valuable lessons. This is attested to, not least, by the fact that his writings contain numerous references to historical figures and events, both Christian and secular. So what lessons can a study of the preaching of this theological giant, born 400 years ago, teach us today?[1]

One approach would be to read his sermons according to what Carl Trueman has described as the 'godly-hero paradigm.'[2] There is surely a place for the kind of approach exemplified by J.I. Packer in his chapter from *Among God's Giants* entitled 'Puritan Preaching.'[3] However, there are significant dangers associated with this method, and it is all too easy to study the past in an anachronistic manner, unwittingly smuggling in all sorts of wrong assumptions and stereotypes.[4] This can so easily stray into some of the worst excesses of hagiography in which history is simply plundered for worthy examples in support of any given position. Crawford Gribben has shown how Owen's legacy has been constantly 'reinvented' by various movements who have found him to be 'a tool for their self-fashioning.'[5]

---

[1] I wish to thank Lee Gatiss and Michael McClenahan for many stimulating conversations about Owen and for their helpful comments in preparation of this lecture.

[2] Carl R. Trueman, *Histories and Fallacies: Problems Faced in the Writing of History* (Wheaton: Crossway, 2010), p 64.

[3] J.I. Packer, in *Among God's Giants: The Puritan Vision of the Christian Life* (Eastbourne: Kingsway, 1991), pp 365-382; R. Bruce Bickel, *Light and Heat: The Puritan View of the Pulpit* (Morgan: Soli Deo Gloria, 1999); Mariano Di Gangi, *Great Themes in Puritan Preaching* (Ontario: Joshua Press, 2007); Joel R. Beeke and Mark Jones, *A Puritan Theology: Doctrine for Life* (Grand Rapids: Reformation Heritage Books, 2012), pp 681-724.

[4] Richard A. Muller, 'Reflections on Persistent Whiggism and its Antidotes in the Study of Sixteenth- and Seventeenth-Century Intellectual History,' in Alister Chapman, John Coffey and Brad S. Gregory, eds., *Seeing Things Their Way: Intellectual History and the Return of Religion* (Notre Dame: University of Notre Dame Press, 2009), p 150.

[5] Crawford Gribben, *John Owen and English Puritanism: Experiences of Defeat* (New York: OUP, 2016), pp 271-273.

In order to explore the legacy of Owen's preaching in a manner that he himself might recognise, the famous quip of L.P. Hartley is apt: 'The past is a foreign country: they do things differently there.'[6] Consequently, to learn from any historical figure we must cultivate the art of listening carefully—only then will we hear the potentially challenging and sometimes subversive messages. So with Owen: rather than airbrush out aspects of his preaching that today might seem unsightly, we will instead paint him according to the instruction given by Cromwell as he sat for a portrait—the man to whom Owen was for a time chaplain insisted that he be painted 'warts and all.' That we sketch Owen in this manner is not at all out of disrespect, but rather, it gives him the honour of taking all steps necessary to hear him on his own terms, rather than superimposing our own agendas. In Owen's preaching we will identify what might be called 'blind spots' in his thinking—ideas that with hindsight have been shown to be patently false. Fascinatingly, it is precisely some of these aberrations that have the greatest power to identify some of the blind spots of those filling modern-day pulpits.

In order to paint this vignette of Owen we will commence by identifying the style of his sermons as an example of later English Puritan preaching, famous for its threefold methodology of doctrine, reason, and use. We will then explain why his preaching through almost forty turbulent years is rightly described as 'prophetic.' First, we will show how, through his understanding of providence and eschatology, Owen believed his hearers to be those who had experienced unique and undeserved divine blessings. Secondly, we will outline how he believed the whole nation, having received such divine favour, was obligated to respond by embracing godly reformation individually, corporately and nationally. Thirdly, we will hear Owen's lamentation as he denounced what he perceived to be consistently negligent responses to his prophetic call. Finally, we will listen to his ominous warnings concerning the signs of a coming divine judgment.

---

[6] L.P. Hartley, *The Go-Between* (1953; London: Penguin, 1958), p 1.

Lessons from the Preaching of John Owen (1616–1683)

Such a portrait may, at first, seem far removed from the impression that many have of Owen as a rather austere scholastic theologian. His dogmatic providentialism and fiery apocalypticism almost threatens to destroy his image as a *Reformed Catholic, Renaissance Man*.[7] With an initial glance, one might think that there was nothing practical that we could learn from this portrait. However we will conclude by exploring three striking applications, or, in the language of early-modern homiletics, 'uses,' that emerge that are directly relevant for much contemporary preaching.

---

[7] Carl R. Trueman, *John Owen: Reformed Catholic, Renaissance Man* (Aldershot: Ashgate, 2007).

2. John Owen's prophetic preaching

Owen's sermons bear all the usual hallmarks of the later English Puritan preaching style.[1] This was part of what Mary Morrissey has termed the 'English Reformed' homiletic method that was structured according the famous tripartite model of text, doctrine, and use.[2] A methodology akin to Owen's is clearly laid out by John Wilkins in his preaching manual *Ecclesiastes* (1646).[3] Wilkins had been a contemporary of Owen's both at Edward Sylvester's private school and in Cromwellian Oxford. Wilkins taught that the 'principal scope of the divine Orator' was to 'Teach clearly. Convince strongly. Persuade powerfully,' and consequently argued that 'the chief parts of a Sermon' are 'Explication. Confirmation. Application.'[4] Thus, in Owen's sermons, we first find him 'opening' the text by carefully exegeting its context, grammar and vocabulary.[5] He then 'divides' the text, a process in which key words and phrases are identified and from which he intends to derive or 'raise' the doctrines that will be expounded. The next element is introduced as Owen states the first of these doctrinal theses in a concise sentence before establishing it by recourse to multiple scriptural proof-texts and supporting reasons e.g. quotations from the Fathers or early modern commentators. In this part of his exposition Owen frequently raises and answers possible objections to the doctrine by way of confirmation. The third element involves him applying the doctrine under consideration according to certain observations of its 'use' (of which there could be several). As

---

[1] Chad B. Van Dixhoorn, 'A Puritan Theology of Preaching' in Lee Gatiss, ed., *Preachers, Pastors, and Ambassadors: Puritan Wisdom for Today's Church: St Antholin Lectures Volume 2: 2001–2010* (London: The Latimer Trust, 2011), pp 205-259.

[2] Mary Morrissey, 'Scripture, Style and Persuasion in Seventeenth-Century English Theories of Preaching,' *Journal of Ecclesiastical History* 53.4 (Oct. 2000), pp 687, 693.

[3] Barbara Shapiro, *John Wilkins 1614–1672: An Intellectual Biography* (Berkeley: University of California Press, 1969).

[4] John Wilkins, *Ecclesiastes* (London, 1647), p 5.

[5] As Gatiss has shown, Owen was an incredibly sophisticated Biblical scholar. See Lee Gatiss, 'Adoring the Fullness of the Scriptures in John Owen's Commentary on Hebrews' (unpublished PhD thesis, University of Cambridge, 2013).

time allowed, this process was repeated for each of the doctrines raised from the text.

Owen's sermons are best described as a form of 'prophetic preaching.'[6] Taking the voices and assuming tropes of the biblical prophets, Owen offered an explanation of the days in which the church found itself and urged his hearers and readers to make a proper response. Patrick Collinson very helpfully summarises the message of this genre as 'always the same: most favoured, more obligated, most negligent.'[7] This pattern is certainly evident in Owen's preaching as he drew attention to the undeserved blessings of apocalyptic significance that the nation had experienced, set forth the obligations incumbent upon it to respond appropriately to this unique providential moment, while lamenting the nation's failures to do so, and warning of the consequent threat of divine judgment. In what follows, we will explore how these four elements are discernible in his sermons even though he is preaching in very different political and religious circumstances.

---

[6] The shorthand of 'prophetic preaching' has been usefully employed by the following scholars: Patrick Collinson, 'Biblical Rhetoric: The English Nation and National Sentiment in the Prophetic Mode,' in Claire McEachern and Debora Shuger, eds., *Religion and Culture in Renaissance England* (Cambridge: Cambridge University Press, 1997), p 27; Mary Morrissey, 'Elect Nations and Prophetic Preaching,' in Lori Anne Ferrell and Peter McCullough, eds., *The English Sermon Revised: Religion, Literature and History 1600–1750* (Manchester: Manchester University Press, 2000), pp 43-58; Daniël Timmerman, *Heinrich Bullinger on Prophecy and the Prophetic Office (1523–1538)* (Göttingen: Vandenhoeck & Ruprecht, 2015).

[7] Collinson, 'Biblical Rhetoric,' p 28.

2.1. Preaching to those uniquely blessed

Throughout his public ministry, John Owen believed that he was preaching in days of unique significance. The events of the mid-seventeenth-century crisis were to him nothing less than an undeserved divine visitation of apocalyptic significance. He was convinced that they would, in time, and if necessary through great suffering, usher in a new heavens and earth, something which he conceived of as an overturning and transformation of both church and state.

In a rare autobiographical note in a short discourse preached to a church meeting in the 1670s he revealed 'it is now towards forty years since God enabled me to observe ... that God had a controversy with the nation.' Such was the significance of the moment for Owen that he described himself awakening 'like a man out of a dead sleep that lifts up his head, and rubs his eyes for a time.'[1] At some stage in the 1630s he awoke with a prophetic worldview that radically transformed his outlook on the English church and nation. What he saw was the widespread influence of Antichrist during the eleven-year tyranny of King Charles' personal reign and in the policies pursued by Archbishop Laud.[2] In his first parliamentary sermon (1646), Owen described how this had been particularly evident in the implementation of liturgical ceremonialism and the rise of doctrinal anti-Calvinism, something he had witnessed first hand in Oxford until the promulgation of the Laudian statutes forced him to leave.[3] For Owen, this alerted him to the fact that the nation stood under God's judgment.[4] He feared that the nation had so 'abused' and 'forsaken' the gospel that it might have forfeited it altogether and he contended that 'The glory of God was of late by many degrees

---

[1] John Owen, *The Works of John Owen*, William H. Goold, ed., 24 vols (Edinburgh: Johnstone and Hunter, 1850-55) vol 9: p 366.

[2] Owen, *Works*, vol 8: p 323.

[3] Gribben, *Owen and English Puritanism*, p 30; Kenneth Fincham, 'Oxford and the Early Stuart Polity,' in Nicholas Tyacke, ed., *The History of the University of Oxford. Vol. 4: Seventeenth-Century Oxford* (Oxford: Clarendon Press, 1997), p 206.

[4] Owen, *Works*, vol 9: p 366

departing from the temple in our land.'[5] Here Owen employs the prophetic tropes of Ezekiel who in a mounting series of vignettes sees the glory of God poised to depart from the midst of a people slowly and by stages because of their idolatry and corrupt government (Ezekiel 8:1–11:25). Owen feared that this Antichristian conspiracy threatened to return the English church to its corrupted, pre-Reformation condition.

He was deeply troubled by the ongoing and widespread effect Laudianism had on the preaching of the English Church whereby 'shepherds may be turned into dumb, sleeping dogs and devouring wolves; the watchmen may be turned smiters, her prophets to prophesy falsely.'[6] Owen clearly was determined to be a true prophet and diligent watchman.

From Owen's perspective, things changed dramatically as he considered some of the events of the Civil War and Interregnum. In 1646 he proclaimed that 'this is the day of England's visitation,' opining that because of God's 'unchangeable free mercy,' the 'house of England' was under 'as full a dispensation of mercy and grace, as ever Nation in the world enjoyed.' He believed that God had broken the Laudian 'snare,' and he claimed that God had set the gospel 'at liberty in England' in an unprecedented manner.[7]

Owen believed that he could identify the '*Digitus Dei*' in the works of providence, pointing to the fact that England was enjoying days of unprecedented blessing.[8] Owen's sermons are replete with references to providentially significant events: the reforms achieved by the Long Parliament in the golden year of 1641;[9] the decisive battle of Naseby; the conclusion of the second Civil War (particularly the relief of the siege of Colchester);[10] the trial and execution of the king; the

---

[5] Owen, *Works*, vol 8: pp 31–32.
[6] Owen, *Works*, vol 13: p 37; vol 2: p 257.
[7] Owen, *Works*, vol 8: pp 1, 6, 30, 38, 40.
[8] Owen, *Works*, vol 8: p 104; vol 9: pp 153, 203; vol 17: p 555.
[9] Owen, *Works*, vol 8: p 411.
[10] Owen, *Works*, vol 8: p 88.

Cromwellian invasion of Ireland;[11] the suppression of the Leveller-inspired mutiny in Burford;[12] the massive Cromwellian victory at Dunbar;[13] the exile of the late king's son after the triumph of the battle of Worcester;[14] and even the capture of part of the cargo of the Spanish plate fleet in 1656.[15]

In his prophetic preaching Owen offered an interpretation of such events by placing them within his very particular eschatological framework. Several biblical images and motifs loom large in his explanation of what he held to be a divine visitation: the 'vengeance of the temple' (Jeremiah 50–51); the measuring of the temple and the restoration of true worship (Revelation 11 and 22); a period of transitional shaking (Hebrews 12); and dissolutions that usher in a new heaven and earth (2 Peter 3). This is vividly captured in a sermon preached to MPs at St Margaret's, Westminster, as part of a nationwide day of fasting in April 1649. His sermon was subsequently published as Οὐρανῶν Οὐρανία: *The Shaking and Translating of Heaven and Earth* (1649). His eschatology led him to believe that the Scottish Presbyterians were serving the cause of Antichrist and that the fifth vial of divine wrath (Revelation 16:10) was being poured out on all forms of episcopalianism.[16]

For Owen, these military, civil and ecclesiastical providences were evidence of the nation receiving unprecedented and undeserved divine blessings of end-times significance. As he told members of the Rump Parliament, 'from the days of old,' there had never been a time when God's 'presence, power and providence' had been seen as clearly.[17]

---

[11] Owen, *Works*, vol 8: p 230.
[12] Owen, *Works*, vol 9: pp 203-04, 213-14.
[13] Owen, *Works*, vol 8: pp 290-91, 303.
[14] Owen, *Works*, vol 8: pp 325, 379.
[15] Owen, *Works*, vol 8: p 432; vol 9: p 308. Bernard S. Capp, *Cromwell's Navy: The Fleet and the English Revolution, 1648–1660* (Oxford: Oxford University Press, 1989), pp 98-99.
[16] Owen, *Works*, vol 8: pp 30, 325, 373.
[17] Owen, *Works*, vol 8: p 313.

2.2. Preaching to those obligated to respond

For Owen, the favour shown to the nation placed great obligation upon the people to respond appropriately. Owen's preaching was a prophetic call for the nation to understand the times and to 'improve' these mercies by comprehensive godly reformation.

Preaching to Parliament at the end of the First Civil War, he told MPs that it would be the height of rebellion to despise the mercies England now enjoyed by being barren and unfruitful in their response. The English 'vineyard' had received such care, culture and watering that great fruit was to be expected.[1] Subsequently, his sermon to 'reluctant regicides,' published as *Righteous Zeal Encouraged by Divine Protection* (1649), urged them to fervent action in light of what God had done.[2] In the sermon *The Stedfastness of the Promises* (1650) Owen called the saints to follow Abraham, setting out in believing obedience, even if they were unsure of exactly where their journey might lead. Then at Henry Ireton's funeral, Owen highlighted how his friend had offered a role model of one who responded to God's 'providential voice' by serving God 'in his Generation.'[3]

As Owen surveyed all the providences of the Puritan Revolution from his study in Christ Church he wrote in the preface to a sermon about how the need for a fruitful response had increased because the nation was now under the greatest 'outward dispensation' of mercy as had been heard of for two thousand years.[4] As he would later explain, the providential 'alterations and dissolutions' were always to be improved by listening to their 'special call.'[5] Owen likened himself to an Old Testament prophet advising the people how to answer that call and make such a fitting improvement.[6] Thus, as Owen surveyed the

---

[1] Owen, *Works*, vol 8: pp 27, 39.
[2] Sean Kelsey, 'The Death of Charles I,' *Historical Journal* 45 (2002): p 754.
[3] Owen, *Works*, vol 8: p 348.
[4] Owen, *Works*, vol 8: pp 313-14.
[5] Owen, *Works*, vol 9: p 137.
[6] Owen, *Works*, vol 8: p 432.

past, his prophetic voice called his generation to respond appropriately by fruitfully improving all such mercies.

The general response required from all professors of religion could be summed up as 'universal holiness.'[7] Developing the motif of 'meeting God,' Owen described this response as going out to 'Meet him in the way of his holiness' or to 'meet him' in 'all holy conversation and godliness.' Owen made clear that this is far beyond the general call to ordinary holiness: this was to be a holiness suitable for those who lived in the dispensation during which Christ came to destroy his Antichristian enemies (Revelation 19:11-12).[8]

Owen argued that those who understood the nature of God's work among them would appreciate that such holiness entailed reformation and separation. In 1658 he explained that one of the works in which Christ was 'peculiarly engaged in our days and seasons' was the 'owning' of his people 'in a distinguishing manner, putting a difference between the precious and the vile.'[9]

This would mean reformation and separation in congregational church polity, gathering a true church of saints who enjoyed genuine communion with God.[10] It also necessitated reformation and separation in the worship of the church, in other words abandoning all forms of idolatry and following a strict regulative principle of worship.[11] Although it is not possible to establish a firm dating of Owen's posthumously-published sermons 'Gospel Worship,' they undoubtedly resonate with the liturgical debates of the 1650s.[12]

Owen and his associates were 'Magisterial' Congregationalists in that they believed that the civil magistrate had an instrumental role in

---

[7] Owen, *Works*, vol 8: p 338; vol 2: pp 187, 205, 266, 308, 320; vol 6: p 4; vol 9: pp 131ff.
[8] Owen, *Works*, vol 8: p 338; vol 9: pp 141, 159-60.
[9] Owen, *Works*, vol 6: p 148.
[10] Owen, *Works*, vol 2: pp 38, 99.
[11] Owen, *Works*, vol 2: pp 150, 268; vol 6: pp 18, 148; vol 8: pp 26, 259, 267, 334; vol 9: p 60.
[12] Owen, *Works*, vol 9: pp 57, 63, 65, 60, 68, 71. Christopher Durston, 'By the Book or With the Spirit: The Debate Over Liturgical Prayer During the English Revolution,' *Historical Research* 79 (2006): pp 50-73.

national reformation.[13] In his preaching Owen called upon those in civil power to implement godly reform in two specific areas. The first was legal reform, and, in this regard, Owen praised parliament's Sabbath laws and urged measures to expedite the execution of justice, particularly those suggested by William Sheppard.[14] A second area of reform called for by Owen was that provision be made for the poor, widows, and orphans (particularly those who had suffered through the war).[15] For Owen, the successful implementation of reform in these areas would have been a fitting response to the divine visitation he believed England to have experienced.

The magistrate also had a role in the search for a church settlement. Owen's first parliamentary sermon was nothing short of a 'Macedonian call' (Acts 16:9). He urged MPs to take upon themselves the task of sending out godly ministers 'acknowledged, owned, and maintained by the supreme magistrate,' especially to Wales and the North of England.[16] Similarly, in 1649 he insisted that it was the government's responsibility to ensure that the gospel be declared to the whole nation.[17] When Owen returned from Cromwell's Irish expedition he took the opportunity in a fast sermon to call MPs to send 'one gospel preacher for every walled town in the English possession in Ireland' and suggested that a committee might be appointed to consider such proposals.[18] At Ireton's high-profile

---

[13] Jeffrey R. Collins, *The Allegiance of Thomas Hobbes* (Oxford: Oxford University Press, 2005), pp 102-14.
[14] Owen, *Works*, vol 8: pp 335, 338, 355, 392, 394, 452; vol 9: p 170. William Sheppard, *Englands Balme: or, Proposals by Way of Grievance and Remedy* (London, 1656); Nancy L. Matthews, *William Sheppard, Cromwell's Law Reformer* (Cambridge: Cambridge University Press, 2004), pp 58, 144-86.
[15] Owen, *Works*, vol 8: pp 148, 355. Judith Richards, 'A "Radical" Problem: The Poor and the English Reformers in the Mid-Seventeenth Century,' *Journal of British Studies* 29 (1990): pp 118-46.
[16] Owen, *Works*, vol 8: pp 7, 40-41, 59. Christopher Hill, 'Puritans and the "Dark Corners of the Land,"' *Transactions of the Royal Historical Society*, 5th Series, 13 (1963): pp 77-102.
[17] Owen, *Works*, vol 8: pp 189, 194.
[18] Owen, *Works*, vol 8: pp 235-37; Blair Worden, *The Rump Parliament 1648-1652* (Cambridge: Cambridge University Press, 1974), pp 120, 234-35.

funeral, Owen continued to urge those with authority to use their 'industry and wisdom' to determine how 'places destitute of the gospel ... might be furnished and supplied.'[19] A week later, Owen and his colleagues submitted a blueprint for a church settlement to the committee.[20] In a sermon from 1652 dealing expressly with the magistrate's power in matters of religion, Owen spoke of how it was incumbent upon MPs that 'the faith,' and 'all the necessary concernments of it,' was 'protected, preserved, propagated.' Elaborating, he called them to ensure that the church was 'supported, and promoted, & the truth propagated.' Equally, he maintained that error and falsehood should not receive any privilege, protection or advantage from the magistrate.[21] Owen would have been delighted when the Rump Parliament appeared to respond to his plea by reviving the Committee for the Propagation of the Gospel.

The call for individuals and churches to 'improve' God's blessings by making a response of fruitful repentant faith and obedient holiness is consistent theme throughout his preaching. Alongside it, and with ever increasing force, there is another characteristic of Owen's prophetic preaching, namely, that his hearers and readers forgot God's mercies and were lax and remiss in their response.

---

[19] Owen, *Works*, vol 8: pp 355-56. Sarah Mortimer, *Reason and Religion in the English Civil War: The Challenge of Socinianism* (Cambridge: Cambridge University Press, 2010), p 198.

[20] *The Humble Proposals of Mr Owen, Mr Tho Goodwin, Mr Nye, Mr Simpson and Other Ministers* (London, 1652).

[21] Owen, *Works*, vol 8: pp 394-96.

2.3. Preaching to those consistently negligent

Like the biblical prophets of old, Owen believed that the nation persistently failed to respond appropriately and he decried what he saw as both individual and national ingratitude, infidelity, and negligence.

Even from his days of parish ministry in Coggeshall, Essex, Owen was particularly troubled by the people's lack of response to his preaching.[1] The lack of response from his own 'provoking people' was highlighted by the reception his preaching received in Ireland. Writing from Dublin Castle in December 1649, Owen described how he was constantly preaching to 'a numerous multitude of as thirsting a people after the Gospel as ever yet I conversed withal.' Indeed, there is evidence that a number of people were converted through his ministry in Ireland.[2]

Some of those that Owen believed to be most negligent were those who had been entrusted with political power. For Owen, the twin temptations of unbelief and pride had caused many of them to backslide from implementing godly reform. The temptation of unbelief received particular attention from Owen in his sermon from February 1650 when he warned MPs that they were staggering and failing to make progress because of their lack of faith.[3] Two years later, in Ireton's funeral sermon, Owen portrayed Ireton as an exemplary godly magistrate precisely because he 'staggered not' but was 'steadfast in faith.'[4] This provided him with the opportunity to caution his hearers to be 'diligent' and not to let the work of reformation 'too long hang upon your hands.'[5] The second major temptation for those in authority was pride.[6] Owen was horrified that

---

[1] Owen, *Works*, vol 1: p 465; vol 8: p 245.
[2] Owen, *Works*, vol 10: p 479; vol 8: p 237. Crawford Gribben, *God's Irishmen: Theological Debates in Cromwellian Ireland* (Oxford: Oxford University Press, 2007), p 26.
[3] Owen, *Works*, vol 8: pp 218-19, 239, 382.
[4] Owen, *Works*, vol 8: pp 351, 359-60.
[5] Owen, *Works*, vol 8: pp 355-56.
[6] Owen, *Works*, vol 8: pp 382, 145-46, 148, 314; vol 9: p 127.

such pride was often, from his perspective, cloaked in religion. He believed that those who were doggedly committed to the Solemn League and Covenant were actually motivated by simple pride.[7]

Owen's posthumously published sermons collected as 'Walking Humbly with God' are undated but they may tentatively be assigned to the period of his preaching in St Mary's, Oxford, sometime from 1653 onwards.[8] Owen reveals his thoughts about the state of his congregation, claiming that among its number were 'empty professors,' the 'profligate,' and 'bitter scoffers, neglecters of ordinances, haters of the power of godliness and the purity of religion.' He detected hostility to his own preaching, especially since the emergence of a 'new-fangled' preaching style that people were 'running after' full of 'novelty' and 'fopperies.' According to Owen, his detractors objected to the reproof that he directed towards them in his preaching and to the manner in which he 'pressed' them about 'this business of a new life.'[9]

Owen's awareness of negligence among his hearers was only to increase. In his two sermons to the second Protectorate Parliament in the autumn of 1656 it is possible to discern the beginning of his alienation from the Cromwellian establishment. He identified those enemies of 'real reformation' as those who were merely 'zealous for the traditions of their fathers' calling for a return to the 'old road.'[10] Further insight into Owen's disillusionment with the regime is gained by assigning a date to another set of Owen's previously undated expository material, published posthumously in 1721 and entitled 'Providential Changes, an Argument for Universal Holiness.'[11] As I have argued elsewhere, these sermons may plausibly

---

[7] Owen, *Works*, vol 8: pp 32, 145-46, 328, 313, 329; vol 9: p 178.
[8] Martyn C. Cowan, 'The Prophetic Preaching of John Owen from 1646 to 1659 in its Historical Context' (unpublished PhD thesis, University of Cambridge, 2012), pp 92-93.
[9] Owen, *Works*, vol 9: p 93.
[10] Owen, *Works*, vol 8: pp 424-25, 452.
[11] Owen, *Works*, vol 9: p 164.

Preaching to those consistently negligent

be dated to 1657.[12] Owen believed that he was addressing a sinfully negligent nation, guilty of a litany of sins. For instance, in only a few lines of the sermon he inveighed against 'unbelief, worldliness, atheism, and contempt of the gospel,' denounced 'swearers, drunkards, and other vicious people' and finally castigated 'The abominable pride, folly, vanity, luxury' of the city.[13] According to Owen, the 'peculiar controversy' that Christ had with the saints was their 'inordinate cleaving unto the shaken, passing things of the world.' Set within the context of the kingship debate, Owen's description of men desiring, 'in things of a public tendency,' that some 'fleshly imagination' be 'enthroned' is striking.[14]

Owen's famous work *Of Temptation* (1658) is based on sermons from Cromwellian Oxford during the time when Owen was losing influence both at Westminster and Oxford. Owen emphasised that these sermons were particularly 'suited to the times that pass over us' in which 'providential dispensations, in reference to the public concernments of these nations' had seen all things 'shaken.'[15] First, it is important to note that Owen was not merely dealing with temptation in a general sense: this was an exposition focused on a particular form of temptation that he likened to the 'hour of temptation' which comes to 'try them that dwell upon the earth' (Revelation 3:10). Owen claimed he was living in a time of 'backsliding' in which 'thousands' had apostatised 'within a few years.'[16] Now increasingly alienated, he highlighted how 'the prevailing party of these nations, many of those in rule, power [and] favour' had formerly been regarded as lowly 'Puritans' but their attitudes had changed once they had been 'translated by a high hand to the mountains they now possess.' Owen lamented: 'how soon they have forgot the customs, manners, ways, of their own old people, and are cast into the mould of them that went before them, in the places

---

[12] Cowan, 'Prophetic Preaching,' pp 112-13.
[13] Owen, *Works*, vol 9: p 158.
[14] Owen, *Works*, vol 9: pp 143, 145-46, 162.
[15] Owen, *Works*, vol 6: pp 89, 150.
[16] Owen, *Works*, vol 6: pp 104, 106.

whereunto they are translated.'[17] He specifically referred to those 'in high places' who were particularly tempted to pursue 'crowns, glories, thrones, pleasures, [and] profits of the world.' Owen's litany of sins resonated with the issues which he believed the Protectorate to be facing: 'setting a value on' the things that Christ 'has stained and trampled under foot'; the 'slighting' of God's people, 'casting them into the same considerations with the men of the world'; and 'leaning to our own counsels.'[18]

As such this is an example of the 'oblique discourse' described by Annabel Patterson by which criticism of contemporary political events was voiced by couching it in Scriptural metaphor. Preachers employed this code of communication 'partly to protect themselves from hostile and hence dangerous readings of their work, partly in order to say what they had to publicly without directly provoking or confronting the authorities.'[19] Not that this was a 'clandestine code': rather, in the early modern sermon 'the biblical idiom was its own and sufficient political comment: a measured, subtle, and precise medium of criticism and a vocabulary of political exordium.'[20]

Given the subversive tenor of Owen's pulpit rhetoric at this time, it was no surprise that in December 1657 it was reported that Owen had been replaced as a preacher at St Mary's. Apparently Owen was greatly displeased and in response had set up a rival Sunday afternoon lecture.[21]

---

[17] Owen, *Works*, vol 6: p 112.
[18] Owen, *Works*, vol 6: pp 105-06, 143, 149.
[19] Annabel M. Patterson, *Censorship and Interpretation: The Conditions of Writing and Reading in Early Modern England* (Madison: University of Wisconsin Press, 1984), pp 10-11, 21.
[20] Kevin J. Killeen, 'Veiled Speech: Preaching, Politics and Scriptural Typology,' in Peter McCullough, Hugh Adlington and Emma Rhatigan, eds., *The Oxford Handbook of the Early Modern Sermon* (Oxford: Oxford University Press, 2011), pp 387-88; Christopher Hill, *The English Bible and the Seventeenth-Century Revolution* (Harmondsworth: Penguin, 1993), p 49.
[21] George Vernon, *A Letter to a Friend Concerning Some of Dr. Owens Principles and Practices* (London, 1670), p 28. Blair Worden, 'Cromwellian Oxford' in Nicholas Tyacke, ed., *The History of the University of Oxford*, vol. 4 (Oxford: Clarendon Press, 1997), p 746.

The series of sermons entitled 'Spiritual Barrenness' may also, tentatively, be dated to 1658 and well sum up his assessment of the lack of a proper fruitful response from his hearers.[22] Recent scholarship concurs, in identifying how, despite some limited success, Interregnum attempts for comprehensive national reformation were a 'dismal failure.'[23] In November 1659, John Locke mocked the dispirited preaching about the state of the nation that he regularly heard from Owen in Christ Church.[24] It would not continue for long, for on 13 March 1660 Parliament removed Owen as Dean.

From Owen's point of view, the Restoration saw yet still more evidence of spiritual declension. He complained that the 'course and lives' of most necessitated that he compile a series of sermons for publications as *The Nature, Power, Deceit and Prevalency of the Remainders of Indwelling Sin* (1668).[25] Throughout the following year, Owen was well aware that he had spoken 'so much and so often' about spiritual 'decay.'[26]

In June 1673, in the aftermath of the failure of the second Declaration of Indulgence, Owen's congregation of around 35 members joined with the larger church that had been pastored by

---

[22] Cowan, 'Prophetic Preaching,' pp 169-70. *Owen, Works*, vol 9: p 188.
[23] Christopher Durston, 'Puritan Rule and the Failure of Cultural Revolution,' in Christopher Durston and Jacqueline Eales, eds., *The Culture of English Puritanism: 1560–1700* (Basingstoke: Macmillan, 1996), pp 210-33; Derek Hurst, 'The Failure of Godly Rule in the English Republic,' *Past and Present* 132 (1991): p 46; Kevin M. Sharpe, *Image Wars: Promoting Kings and Commonwealths in England, 1603–1660* (New Haven: Yale University Press, 2010), pp 465-543. For the limited success see: Elliot Vernon, 'A Ministry of the Gospel: The Presbyterians During the English Revolution,' in Christopher Durston and Judith Maltby, eds., *Religion in Revolutionary England* (Manchester: Manchester University Press, 2006), pp 115-36; Bernard Capp, England's *Culture Wars: Puritan Reformation and its Enemies in the Interregnum, 1649–1660* (Oxford: Oxford University Press, 2012), pp 257-63; Ann Hughes, '"The Public Profession of These Nations": the National Church in Interregnum England' in Durston and Maltby, eds., *Religion*, pp 93-114.
[24] Esmond de Beer, ed., *The Correspondence of John Locke* (Oxford: Clarendon Press, 1976-89), vol 1: pp 83-84.
[25] Owen, *Works*, vol 6: pp 155, 170, 174, 215.
[26] Owen, *Works*, vol 17: pp 587-88, 518.

Joseph Caryl in Leadenhall Street. It became 'one of the most aristocratic of the London Nonconformist congregations.'[27] This was only three months after the failure of the second Declaration of Indulgence and the passing of Parliament's first Test Act that required, amongst other things, all officer-holders under the crown to take communion in the Church of England. Some dissenting Protestants chose to fulfil the requirements of the Test Act by occasional conformity. This was unacceptable to members of Owen's congregation, and so it was not unexpected that in September 1673 the churchwardens of the parish of Stoke Newington presented Sir John Hartopp, his father-in-law, Charles Fleetwood, and their wives 'for not comeing to theire said parish Church nor receiving the sacrament at Easter last past nor since to this day.'[28] In March 1674 Owen reminded his church of what was entailed by the 'vow and covenant' of membership, recalling how in the past separation had resulted in God carrying 'many of his people out of this nation into the wilderness, and they hid them for a season.'[29] This is reference to the flight of the godly to the continent and the new world as a result of Laudian persecution. However, at this point Owen opined: 'I see no ground for that now.'[30]

Early in 1676 the government began a concerted crackdown on dissent, and in February, an informer reported Owen's congregation to be very dangerous, 'praying and preaching to the decrying of the present power and all authority to them contrary.'[31] That year Owen attributed much of this 'general plague' of 'the apostasy of the day wherein we live' to the prevalence of a style of preaching that simply

---

[27] C.E. Whiting, *Studies in English Puritanism* (London: SPCK, 1931), p 78. For a list of the members see T.G. Crippen, 'Dr Watts's church-book,' *Congregational Historical Society Transactions*, 1 (1901–4): pp 26-38.

[28] Trevor Cliffe, *The Puritan Gentry Besieged 1650–1700* (London: Routledge, 2002), p 84; Guildhall Library, London, Diocese of London Records, Episcopal visitation Books, MS 9683/2, part VI, fo. 69.

[29] Owen, *Works*, vol 9: p 293.

[30] Owen, *Works*, vol 9: p 295.

[31] Richard L. Greaves, *Enemies Under his Feet: Radicals and Nonconformists in Britain 1664–1677* (Stanford: Stanford University Press, 1990), p 128; CSPD 1675–76, p 571.

dealt with 'virtue and vice.'[32] In contrast, at that time Owen was resolved to preach 'plainly and familiarly' about the present 'infirmities' of the church in order to discharge his duties as a prophetic watchman (Ezekiel 33).[33] He was concerned that the 'efficacy of the truth' was beginning to 'decay,' and he singled out 'God's eternal election' and 'justification by the imputation of the righteousness of Christ' as doctrines about which his generation had become indifferent.[34] According to Owen, the great need for that 'season' was for the godly to 'Labour for the experience of the power of every truth in your own hearts and lives.'[35] Surveying the Restoration Church, he urged his hearers not to be 'half Arminian and half Socinian, half Papist and half I know not what.'[36]

In the preface to *The Doctrine of Justification* (1677) Owen articulated his fear that the whole country was creeping into apostasy, bemoaning the existence of 'a horrible decay in true gospel purity and holiness of life among the generality of men.'[37] In the years that followed he continued to despair at the lack of fruit and 'the decay of love' and the 'withering' and 'decay' of spiritual life.[38] In May 1680 his assessment of the 'general declension in religion' was that it was a 'time of decay among us, amongst churches, amongst church-members, and professors of all sorts and ways throughout this nation ... and the neighbouring nations.'[39] After contemplating his own death during an illness, he published the thoughts he had shared with 'a private congregation' as *The Grace and Duty of being Spiritually Minded* (1681). These revealed his concern about a 'worldly frame of spirit in many who make profession of religion.'[40]

---

[32] Owen, *Works*, vol 9: pp 368-69.
[33] Owen, *Works*, vol 9: p 320.
[34] Owen, *Works*, vol 9: p 326.
[35] Owen, *Works*, vol 9: p 328.
[36] Owen, *Works*, vol 9: p 329.
[37] Owen, *Works*, vol 5: p 5.
[38] Owen, *Works*, vol 17: p 547; vol 9: p 343.
[39] Owen, *Works*, vol 9: pp 510-11.
[40] Owen, *Works*, vol 7: p 264.

By now Owen was weary, telling his congregation: 'I have now been very long, though very unprofitable, in the ministration of the word.... I am ready to faint, and give over, and to beg of the church they would think of some other person to conduct them in my room.'[41] In 1681 he issued 'the substance of sundry sermons preached in a private congregation' as *An Humble Testimony unto the Goodness and Severity of God* (1681).[42] His text was Luke 13:1-5 that recounted the murder of the Galileans 'whose blood Pilate had mingled with their sacrifices' and the tragedy of the eighteen killed when the tower in Siloam fell. On the title page was the text 'Cry aloud, spare not, lift up thy voice like a trumpet, and shew my people their transgression, and the house of Jacob their sins' (Isaiah 58:1). Owen was concerned about the deep divisions within society as well as external threats to the nation's security and went on to advocate repentance and 'universal Reformation' as the only response.[43]

On 30 September 1681, so intense was the 'time of persecution' that Owen witnessed 'a time of great decays in all churches' and 'the ruin of many professors.'[44] A month later, on 29 October, magistrates were again ordered to clamp down on conventicles.[45] By the end of November charges had been issued against Owen and ten other dissenting ministers for recusancy and violating the Five-Mile Act for which they reportedly faced possible cumulative fines of £4,840. A subsequent list, prepared in December, named Owen alongside twenty-one other ministers with outstanding fines of £9,680.[46]

In the early months of 1682 Owen's sermons evinced his reaction to the growing persecution.[47] In February he told his congregation to

---

[41] Owen, *Works*, vol 9: p 405.
[42] Owen, *Works*, vol 8: p 595.
[43] Owen, *Works*, vol 8: p 643
[44] Owen, *Works*, vol 9: pp 352-53, 356.
[45] *True Protestant Mercury* 86 (29 October–2 November 1681).
[46] *CSPD 1680–81*, pp 592-660; *HMC Reports 36 Ormonde*, NS, vol 6: pp 229, 242, 244; Narcissus Luttrell, *A Brief Historical Relation of State Affairs from September 1678 to April 1714*, 6 vols. (Oxford: Oxford University Press, 1857), vol 1: p 148.
[47] Dr Williams's Library (DWL), MSS L6/3.

wait patiently and quietly as God imposed his judgment. The following week, on 19 February, a JP dispatched three observers to Owen's conventicle.[48] In May 1682 he told the congregation that suffering should be regarded as commonplace. In June he distinguished between 'the prophane, hypocritical, persecuting Church, and ... the Church of the Elect.'[49] The implications for those tempted to occasional conformity would have been clear. As the year went on, coercion escalated and, by the autumn, the Hilton gang claimed to have a network of more than fifty men searching for conventicles in the London area and to have obtained convictions in the preceding six months resulting in fines in excess of £17,000.[50] On Thursday 26 October Owen and other ministers were indicted.[51] At the end of the year he urged his followers not to yield to demands for conformity, arguing that it would only make matters worse for other dissenters and mar the godly reputation of those who had suffered in the past for nonconformity.[52] Subsequently, on 19 April 1683, the grand jury for the City of London presented seventeen ministers, including Owen, for preaching at conventicles.[53]

---

[48] National Archives, State Papers, 29/418/106, 127. Mark Goldie, 'The Hilton Gang and the Purge of London in the 1680s,' in Howard Nenner, ed., *Politics and the Political Imagination in Later Stuart Britain* (Rochester: University of Rochester Press, 1997), p 48.
[49] DWL, MSS L6/3.
[50] Luttrell, vol 1: pp 213, 216, 229. This gang had over forty members (including at least fifteen women) and it was responsible for breaking up more than forty conventicles.
[51] Luttrell, vol 1: pp 230, 232, 237.
[52] DWL, MSS L6/4.
[53] Richard L. Greaves, *Glimpses of Glory: John Bunyan and English Dissent* (Stanford: Stanford University Press, 2002), p 459; *The Presentment for the City of London at the Sessions of Peace and Gaol Delivery* (1683), pp 2-3.

2.4. Preaching to those warned by judgment

Owen warned such a sinfully negligent nation and government about the threat of divine judgment. By means of the 'Israelite paradigm' Owen applied the warnings of the Old Testament prophets to the nation. It has been noted that such preaching during the Civil War and Interregnum was 'the climax' of a century of English Hoseads and Jeremiads.[1] For Owen, England was like Israel because she was a chosen and visited land which had witnessed many glorious providences and yet, despite these unparalleled blessings, had failed to respond appropriately.[2]

Owen portrayed England's position as particularly precarious. In 1646 he outlined how, he believed, England had historically been spiritually unfruitful. Using the biblical motif of the unfruitful vineyard, Owen spoke of two previous times when a divine visitation had found only 'wild grapes' and because of which the land had forfeited the gospel. The first was that lamented by 'doleful' Gildas in preaching against the national degeneracy of the Britons in the sixth century and the second was when the Antichristian apostasy 'left the land in little less than pagan darkness.' Nevertheless, like Israel of old, the nation was revived, in this case, by the coming of the Protestant Reformation. Owen cautioned that since every provision had now been made for the plant to produce fruit, if upon a third visitation it was found to be fruitless, it would be cut down and burned. Therefore, he entreated England to consider with fear and

---

[1] Collinson, 'Biblical Rhetoric,' pp 27-28. For the background of the seventeenth-century jeremiad, see: James Egan, '"This is a Lamentation and shall be for a Lamentation": Nathaniel Ward and the Rhetoric of the Jeremiad,' *Proceedings of the American Philosophical Society* 122 (1978): pp 400-10; Laura Lunger Knoppers, 'Milton's The Readie and Easie Way and the English Jeremiad,' in David Loewenstein and James Grantham Turner, eds., *Politics, Poetics and Hermeneutics in Milton's Prose* (Cambridge: Cambridge University Press, 1990), pp 213-25; Michael McGiffert, 'God's Controversy with Jacobean England' in *The American Historical Review* 88 (1983): pp 1152-1153; Morrissey, 'Elect Nations,' pp 43-58.

[2] Owen, *Works*, vol 6: p 89.

trembling the dispensation that it was now under, rather bluntly stipulating: 'mend or end.'[3]

At the end of the Second Civil War he was left pondering 'what will be the issue of the visitations of the last years,' remembering how history had revealed that when God intends the total destruction of a people he often weakens them with previous judgments such as those they had just experienced.[4] Months later, he claimed that the nation had been 'eminently sick of the folly of backsliding' for the past three years—in effect since the fracturing of the parliamentary cause in the early months of 1646. Ominously, he asserted that England had now fallen three times and thus, without renewal, it was inevitable that, as an 'empty vine,' the nation was destined for the flames.[5]

In April 1649, at a fast held 'to implore God's forgiveness for the ingratitude of the people,' Owen outlined 'The dangerous and pernicious consequence of backsliding,' telling MPs to 'tremble' and 'search your hearts' because the nation was about to enter 'the most purging, trying furnace that ever the Lord set up on the earth.'[6] A year later, he warned Parliament to repent of fleshly reasoning and carnal contrivances 'before it be too late.'[7] At Ireton's funeral, Owen drew attention to how the death of the godly should be viewed as a warning since God often removed significant individuals (often either ministers or magistrates) before a coming judgment.[8] Months later, in October 1652, he urged the implementation of reform, telling MPs that they had 'certainly backslidden.' Charging them to 'renew your old frame,' he told them starkly: 'The rejection of the Gospel by any people or nation to whom it is tendered is always attended with the certain and inevitable destruction of that people or nation.'[9]

---

[3] Owen, *Works*, vol 8: pp 26, 31.
[4] Owen, *Works*, vol 8: p 92.
[5] Owen, *Works*, vol 2: p 41; vol 8: pp 32, 138, 143; vol 9: p 164.
[6] Owen, *Works*, vol 8: pp 249, 279.
[7] Owen, *Works*, vol 8: pp 240-41.
[8] Owen, *Works*, vol 8: p 356.
[9] Owen, *Works*, vol 8: p 385.

The frequency of these warnings would only increase. In 'Providential Changes,' Owen continued to lament the 'general backsliding of most, if not of all, professors,' and on three occasions made reference to his contention that Christ had a 'controversy with these nations.' Such provocations were, he believed, enough for God 'to forsake the work on the wheel.' This was a reference to Jeremiah's description of a potter refusing to rework the vessel as symbolising a nation being prepared for destruction (Jeremiah 18:4,10).[10] Those who heard the allusion would remember that in the following chapter Jeremiah shattered a clay flask as a sign of judgment coming upon the nation (Jeremiah 19:1,10).

The series of sermons collected under the title 'Spiritual Barrenness' may, we have argued, be tentatively dated to 1658. Owen's prognosis was that 'Sad symptoms appear of a tremendous issue' in this 'special season' in which 'providential calls do join in with, and further, gospel calls.'[11] Owen pondered over what would be the outcome of 'England's enjoying the gospel so long as it hath done' given the high-handed provocation and spiritual backsliding which he observed. Like the prophet Ezekiel, he identified signs or 'tokens' of God's wrath against the nation, including sickness, conflict and extreme weather (Ezekiel 38:22). His assessment was that God had a controversy with the nation.[12] The healing waters of the preaching of the gospel had, like the waters from Ezekiel's temple, been flowing over the land for an allotted 'season of healing.' He warned that if repeatedly rejected, these 'waters of the sanctuary' would eventually cease to flow and the land would be 'given up, by the righteous judgment of God, unto barrenness and everlasting ruin': 'the miry places thereof, and the marshes thereof shall not be healed; they shall be given to salt' (Ezekiel 47:11).[13]

In his February 1659 fast sermon to Richard's Parliament, Owen spoke of how, despite the 'outward peace' that the nation enjoyed,

---

[10] Owen, *Works*, vol 9: pp 146, 158, 164, 176, 178.
[11] Owen, *Works*, vol 9: pp 182, 195.
[12] Owen, *Works*, vol 9: pp 182, 142, 192-93; vol 8: p 92.
[13] Owen, *Works*, vol 9: p 181.

there was evidence that all was not well because he identified symptoms of 'a profane, wicked, [and] carnal spirit.'[14] In what must be seen as an indictment of the current Protectorate, he described how 'the temptations of these days' had led to a return to 'old forms and ways' which Owen regarded as 'a badge of apostasy' from 'our good old principles on which we first engaged.' He feared lest 'our ruin should come with more speed than did our deliverance' and that the nation would 'quickly return to its former station and condition, and that with the price of your dearest blood.'[15] He employed an apt metaphor from Hosea to describe the state of the nation: 'Gray hairs and here' and he knows it not (Hosea 7:9). In other words, England was like a man unaware that he had suddenly grown old, weak, and near death.[16] Similarly, drawing upon the Oracle of Doom from Amos 4:1-13, he expressed his fear that, despite providential warnings, the glory was departing. The only hope, as he saw it, would be for England's leaders to make 'the preservation of the interest of Christ ... the great thing in their eyes.'[17] Ominously, in the weeks that followed Owen saw little evidence of the repentance and reformation he desired.

With the Restoration, much of the providentialism and apocalypticism of his earlier years disappears from what he sent to the printing press. However, we know from his posthumously published and unpublished sermons that Owen's preaching continued in the same prophetic mould. In what Gribben has described as one of his 'strategies for survival,' 'Owen was increasingly distinguishing the private voice of the prophet from the public voice of the scribe.'[18]

---

[14] Owen, *Works*, vol 8: p 467. For the context see Derek Hirst, 'Concord and Discord in Richard Cromwell's House of Commons,' *English Historical Review* 103 (1988): pp 339-58.
[15] Owen, *Works*, vol 8: pp 467-68.
[16] Jeremiah Burroughes, *Fourth, Fifth, Sixth, and Seventh Chapters of the Prophesy of Hosea* (London, 1650), p 679.
[17] Owen, *Works*, vol 8: pp 466-67.
[18] Gribben, *John Owen and English Puritanism*, p 238.

In 'The Furnace of Divine Wrath,' Owen lamented people's unresponsiveness to the great comet, the plague and the great fire (1664–1666): 'The plague, the fire, have not done it; signs in heavens above and in the earth beneath have not done it; the sincere preaching of the gospel, though in weakness, hath not done it; entreaties, beggings, exhortations, hath not done it.'[19] Consequently, as he had been warning those attending his conventicle 'for some years,' they were all 'going into the same furnace.'[20]

Owen's impassioned prophetic warnings continued. In a sermon on Friday 11 July 1673 he prayed that his church might 'be awakened to a diligent watchfulness' because of 'the signs and tokens of an approaching dissolution' that had included the great fire of London and the plague.[21] In March 1674 he voiced a fear of God sending judgment in the form of a return to Popery because of the sins that had reigned 'for a long season' in 'the nation at this day.'[22] The following year he threatened that God might withdraw his presence in order to correct the wayward church.[23] And he warned of 'perilous times,' mentioning again the judgement of the plague, the fire and also 'inundations.'[24] At a fast on New Year's Day 1676 Owen spoke of God hiding his face and attributed it to 'a non-compliance with the calls of providence.'[25] In November he warned the church of the 'present perilous times' in which they were living. He thought his preaching had made little impact, describing it as 'poor,' 'weak' and 'quickly forgotten.'[26] At this solemn day of fasting and prayer, Owen lamenting that his people were unmoved by the sins that had 'provoked' God, solemnly informed them that 'There is no one of us

---

[19] Owen, *Works*, vol 17: p 496; William E. Burns, *An Age of Wonders: Prodigies, Politics, and Providence in England 1657-1727* (Manchester: Manchester University Press, 2002), p 98.
[20] Owen, *Works*, vol 17: p 493.
[21] Owen, *Works*, vol 17: p 530.
[22] Owen, *Works*, vol 9: p 294.
[23] Owen, *Works*, vol 9: p 296.
[24] Owen, *Works*, vol 9: p 299.
[25] Owen, *Works*, vol 17: p 593.
[26] Owen, *Works*, vol 9: p 332.

can have any evidence that we shall escape outward judgements that God will bring for these abominations.'[27] Reminding them of the 'dreadful' plague and fire of the previous decade, Owen explained that 'We do not prophesy of things a great way off; no, we shall speak of things that are even upon us,—what we see and know, and is as evident as if written with the beams of sun.'[28]

In 1677 the Lord Mayor was instructed to suppress conventicles in the City.[29] On 18 October 1677, Owen's sermon on the power of God's anger (Psalm 90:11) revealed that he anticipated a period of major persecution: 'I am persuaded, Brethren, the day is coming, the day is nowe at hand, wherein you will stand in need of all the Experiences that ever you had of the Presence of God with you, and his Protection of you.'[30] The following year he pondered whether the men and women 'in the Assemblye of Gods People, be Fitt to meet the Lord in the Way of his Judgmente.'[31]

In early 1679 public opinion was still dominated by allegations of a popish plot and this increased anti-Catholic hostility and led to demands to exclude the Duke of York from the succession.[32] Just in time for the first so-called Exclusion Parliament, Owen issued two of his sermons under the title *The Church of Rome no Safe Guide* (1679).[33] On 11 April Owen expounded Isaiah 3:8-9 to a 'ruined' and 'dying nation' in the sermon collected as 'National Sins and National Judgments.' Sir John Hartopp arrived late and Owen called the congregation to remember the warnings of 'signs in the heavens above' and the death of godly men, as well as the plague and fire,

---

[27] Owen, *Works*, vol 9: p 325.
[28] Owen, *Works*, vol 9: pp 323, 327.
[29] CSPD 1676–77, p 547.
[30] DWL, MSS L6/3.
[31] DWL, MSS L6/3.
[32] John P. Kenyon, *The Popish Plot* (London, William Heinemann, 1972), p 239.
[33] Owen, *Works*, vol 14: p 481. See John Miller, *Popery and Politics in England 1660–1688* (Cambridge: Cambridge University Press, 1973), p 174.

predicting that 'London will be undone and England will fall.'[34] This was a nationwide day of humiliation to ask for God's forgiveness and his help to defeat the nation's enemies. At a church meeting on 5 December 1679, Owen spoke of a day of 'great Triall, of great Temptations, of great Dangers' and so recommended (unsuccessfully) that the congregation renew its church covenant.[35] On Thursday 8 January 1680, Owen once again preached about renewing the church covenant, telling his congregation that all the ministers with whom he was conversing thought God was about to impose a period of darkness on England, disagreeing only on its length.[36]

During April and May 1680, Owen preached four sermons on *The Use of Faith* from Habakkuk 2:4 and in them surveyed the spectre of a return of Roman Catholicism.[37] He spoke of the general declension in religion and, observing the gathering storm clouds, told his church that he had been reminding them for many years and 'warning you continually of an approaching calamitous time, and considering the sins that have been the cause of it.'[38]

Owen's fast day sermon from Jeremiah 51:5 was preached during the second Exclusion Parliament (22 December 1680) and was later published as *Seasonable Words for English Protestants* (1690).[39] Owen asked what the 'greatest aggravations' were to 'national sins.' For him the answer was 'plain'—those sins committed 'against all sorts of warnings and against all sorts of mercies.'[40] Noting that some preaching had been weak in sounding a note of warning, Owen adopted the posture of the Biblical prophet, making reference to the

---

[34] Owen, *Works*, vol 17: p 550. The cover illustration depicts an unknown minister preaching a fast sermon in London on 11 April 1679.
[35] DWL, MSS L6/4.
[36] DWL, MSS L6/4.
[37] Owen, *Works*, vol 9: p 505.
[38] Owen, *Works*, vol 9: pp 491, 499.
[39] Owen, *Works*, vol 9: p 2. For the dating see Gribben, *John Owen and English Puritanism*, pp 257, 345.
[40] Owen, *Works*, vol 9: p 10.

plague, the fire, the second Dutch war and 'the prodigious appearances in heaven above.'[41] The latter is a reference to the great comet that appeared in November 1680 and stayed in the sky until the end of March.[42] Owen believed that there was still time to heed these warnings, believing that the discovery of the alleged Popish Plot was a token of divine mercy indicating that 'England is not yet ... utterly forsaken of the Lord.'[43] Owen explained how since the discovery of the Plot, and through the ensuing Restoration Crisis, he had constantly been warning about judgment. He was confident that the congregation 'know my mind full well in this matter' since 'for these last three years' he had 'upon all occasions' been exposing the sins of 'churches and professors in this nation' and warning that 'Christ will bring correcting judgments upon churches and professors.'[44]

In March 1682 he again predicted that public calamities would befall the church.[45] The plight of dissenters worsened in the summer after the election of a new Tory Lord Mayor and new Tory sheriffs. In September Owen pondered 'Where is the man of Wisdome now to save the Citty?'[46]

Owen's own death was near, but his prophetic hope remained strong. In the year before his death he pointedly warned that 'princes' who reconciled with Rome would 'bring Bondage on themselves and

---

[41] Owen, *Works*, vol 9: p 11.
[42] Eric G. Forbes, 'The Comet of 1680–1681,' in Norman J.W. Thrower, ed., *Standing on the Shoulders of Giants: A Longer View of Newton and Halley* (Berkeley: University of California Press, 1990), pp 312-323. Sara J. Schechner, *Comets, Popular Culture, and the Birth of Modern Cosmology* (Princeton: Princeton University Press, 1997), p 76.
[43] Owen, *Works*, vol 9: p 13.
[44] Owen, *Works*, 9: p 10.
[45] DWL, MSS L6/3.
[46] DWL, MSS L6/3. John R. Woodhead, *The Rulers of London 1660–1689* (London and Middlesex Archaeological Society, 1965), pp 44, 77, 125, 130; Gary S. De Krey, 'Radicals, Reformers, and Republicans Academic Language and Political Discourse in Restoration London,' in Alan Houston and Steve Pincus, eds., *A Nation Transformed: England After the Restoration* (Cambridge: Cambridge University Press, 2001), p 96.

their subjects.'[47] However, he concluded this treatise with the confident assertion that 'Antichrist shall not be a final gainer in this contest; his success herein will be a forerunner of his utter destruction. The healing of his deadly wound will preserve his life but for a little while. Religion shall again be restored in a more refined profession.'[48]

---

[47] Owen, *Works*, vol 14: p 549.
[48] Owen, *Works*, vol 14: p 555.

3. Conclusion

We have ranged far and wide with Owen, having tried to hear him preach, as it were, to the political elites at Westminster (from St Margaret's and the Abbey), as an army chaplain on foreign soil (in Ireland and Scotland), to students and academics at the University of Oxford (from St Mary's and Christ Church) and also from the conventicle pulpit with informers in the congregation and legal action hanging over him. As we have strained to hear him across the centuries, both the form and the content of his preaching are unfamiliar to the modern ear. His hermeneutical approach to both the text of Scripture and his own socio-political context is at times shocking, particularly because of the pervasive influence of a historicist millenarian eschatology that the passage of time has discredited. Furthermore, it would be impossible to replicate his homiletical method that produced such lengthy and structurally sophisticated sermons in our contemporary context. The past really is 'a foreign country' where 'they do things differently.' Having travelled such a distance, upon our return to home, we will inevitably experience some reverse culture shock.

The particular emphases of Owen's preaching illuminate several significant shortcomings in some contemporary preaching. Some of the distinctives of his preaching that sound most dissonant in our ears contain within them lessons that need to be heard.

First, the corporate application of Owen's preaching makes the individualism of so much modern preaching stand out in stark relief. Owen preaches to the nation and to churches as corporate entities and not simply to isolated individuals. Charles Taylor has identified Western individualism as one of the 'malaises of modernity.'[1] In Owen's early-modern preaching we hear a prophetic voice alerting us to how the church now so often simply seems to reflect the pervasive individualism of the culture rather than challenge it. And even when

---

[1] For the rise of individualism see Charles Taylor, *Sources of the Self: The Making of the Modern Identity* (Cambridge: Cambridge University Press, 1989).

the congregational application of preaching is taken seriously, Owen's example reminds us of how a preacher may address his auditors not simply as members of the congregation, but also as citizens of the nation.

Secondly, the ever-present providentialism within Owen's sermons reveals how, following the Enlightenment, a robust doctrine of providence has been replaced by a secular view of history that is either cynical about the whole idea of history or has replaced providence with a vague, impersonal law of linear progress.[2] Undoubtedly, the hubris that marked the interpretation of providence by Owen and others like him was a factor that promoted that process of decline. All that being said, if our preaching makes no careful and judicious attempts to interpret providence then the people of God will be impoverished. There still are national and congregational, familial and individual blessings that ought to be, in Owen's language, improved and there are similar types of warnings whose call must be heeded.

Finally, in Owen we readily see what a pervasive influence one's eschatology can exercise over every aspect of thought and practice. It is a mistake to think that eschatology may be treated as a discrete isolated area of doctrine of, perhaps, only secondary importance. In Owen we see how a preacher may be enthused and emboldened by his end-times convictions and consequently persevere even in the face of opposition and government-sponsored hostility. In the light of this, we should endeavour to have our own end-times realities permeate and shape every aspect of doctrinal and biblical-theological reflection and every aspect of pastoral ministry.[3]

---

[2] John Webster, 'Providence,' in Kelly M. Kapic and Bruce L. McCormack, eds., *Mapping Modern Theology: A Thematic and Historical Introduction* (Grand Rapids: Baker, 2012), p 209; Genevieve Lloyd, *Providence Lost* (Cambridge, MA: Harvard University Press, 2008); R.G. Collingwood, *The Idea of History* (Oxford: Clarendon Press, 1964), p 79; Owen Chadwick, *The Secularization of the European Mind in the Nineteenth Century* (Cambridge: Cambridge University Press, 1990), p 262.

[3] See the excellent application of eschatology to pastoral ministry by Benjamin L. Gladd and Matthew S. Harmon, *Making all Things New: Inaugurated Eschatology for the Life of the Church* (Grand Rapids: Baker, 2016), particularly pp 76-77, 94-95.

Conclusion

If our preaching was less individualistic, recovered the application of providence and declared more of the end-times realities of the gospel then it would surely speak with greater prophetic clarity to our own days. May we, and many others, be roused from our slumbers to see that, despite our tremendous Christian heritage, God still has a controversy with this nation. The only appropriate response is for gospel preachers to stand as watchmen calling individuals, churches and the nation, to sincere repentance and genuine reformation.